STAR WARS

THE CLONE WARS

THE COLOSSUS OF DESTINY

DESIGNER **KRYSTAL HENNES**

ASSISTANT EDITOR **FREDDYE LINS**

EDITOR **RANDY STRADLEY**

PUBLISHER **MIKE RICHARDSON**

Special thanks to Troy Alders, Jann Moorhead, David Anderman, Leland Chee, Sue Rostoni, and Carol Roeder at Lucas Licensing.

STAR WARS: CLONE WARS - THE COLOSSUS OF DESTINY

ISBN: 9781848565371

Published by Titan Books, a division of Titan Publishing Group Ltd.
144 Southwark Road, London SE1 0UP

Originally published by Dark Horse Comics.

A CIP catalogue record for this title is available from the British Library.

First edition: February 2010

10 9 8 7 6 5 4 3 2 1

Printed in Lithuania

The events in this story take place sometime during the Clone Wars.

STAR WARS
THE CLONE WARS

THE COLOSSUS OF DESTINY

SCRIPT **JEREMY BARLOW** ART **THE FILLBACH BROTHERS**

COLOURS **RONDA PATTISON** LETTERING **MICHAEL HEISLER**

COVER ART **WAYNE LO**

TITAN BOOKS

THIS STORY TAKES PLACE WITHIN THE FIRST YEAR OF THE CLONE WARS.

WHAT WOULD YOU HAVE ME DO, *MASTER YODA*--

--TURN MY BACK ON AN ENTIRE WORLD? ON MY *FRIENDS?*

OF COURSE NOT. BUT RIGHT NOW NEEDED ELSEWHERE, YOU ARE.

WORRY I DO THAT *CLOUDED* YOUR JUDGMENT HAS BECOME.

CLOUDED? YOU KNOW ME BETTER THAN THAT.

WITH RESPECT, MASTER-- I APPRECIATE YOUR CONCERN, BUT IT'S TOO LATE...

...I'M ALREADY ON MY WAY.

IN ORBIT ABOVE **SIMOCADIA**, IN THE INNER RIM.

MACE DOESN'T WANT TO ADMIT IT...BUT YODA MIGHT BE RIGHT.

MAYBE HE **ISN'T** THINKING CLEARLY.

AS A JEDI, HE'S TRAINED TO KEEP HIS EMOTIONS IN CHECK...

HE KNOWS HE SHOULDN'T LET HIS CONCERN FOR A SINGLE WORLD OVERRULE HIS RESPONSIBILITIES TO THE REPUBLIC...

PISH!

...BUT SIMOCADIA ISN'T JUST ANY WORLD. NOT TO MACE, IT ISN'T.

UNFORTUNATELY, THE REST OF THE GALAXY HAS TAKEN NOTICE OF IT AS WELL.

SEIZE THE PALACE!

WE CAN'T HOLD THEM BACK!

WHERE IS THE REPUBLIC SUPPORT?!

EMPRESS SEPHANI -- OUR DEFENSES ARE FAILING!

WE HAVE TO GET YOU TO THE TUNNELS BEFORE IT'S TOO LATE!

NO, TOBIN... IT'S ALREADY TOO LATE.

HURRY, YOJAN -- HURRY, MY SON...

A FEW KILOMETERS AWAY...

DO YOU SEE THAT?

I DON'T NEED TO. WE HAVEN'T MUCH TIME.

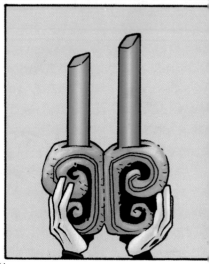

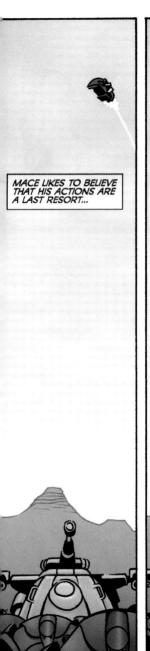

MACE LIKES TO BELIEVE THAT HIS ACTIONS ARE A LAST RESORT...

...THAT THE CONFEDERACY OF INDEPENDENT SYSTEMS'S INVASION OF SIMOCADIA FORCED THE REPUBLIC'S HAND --

-- FORCED *HIS* HAND -- INTO CHOOSING COMBAT OVER DIPLOMACY...

...BUT THE TRUTH ISN'T SO SIMPLE.

SKA-KRASH!

THE TRUTH IS MACE *LIKES* THIS.

KSSH! KSSH! KSSH!

THE TRUTH IS THAT SOMETIMES ONLY THE RHYTHMS OF BATTLE CAN SOOTHE THE STORM OF CONFLICTING EMOTIONS THAT SWIRL DEEP WITHIN HIM.

IT'S NOT A VERY JEDI-LIKE QUALITY, HE KNOWS...

...BUT IN TIMES LIKE THESE...IS THAT SUCH A BAD THING?

WE GOT YOUR MESSAGE, GENERAL WINDU -- SORRY WE'RE LATE.

TRY TO SAVE SOME OF THOSE DROIDS FOR US!

NO PROMISES, PONDS.

WE NEED TO PROTECT THE EMPRESS'S PALACE -- TAKE YOUR SQUADRON AHEAD AND I'LL MEET YOU THERE.

COPY THAT, SIR.

AND SO MACE PRESSES EVER FORWARD, LOSING HIMSELF IN THE FLOW OF WARFARE...

...REMEMBERING THE LAST TIME HE CAME TO SIMOCADIA'S RESCUE AND WONDERING HOW MUCH HAS REALLY CHANGED SINCE...

Legend tells of a young warrior who fell from the stars during our darkest hour.

He faced an army of invading demons, ten thousand strong -- not yet knowing that his might ALONE would not be enough...

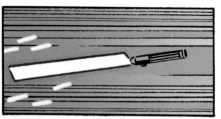

YOU DROIDS SURE YOU STILL WANT TO GO THROUGH WITH THIS?

I'M NOT PROGRAMMED TO SURRENDER, ARE YOU?

....

WZWAAMM!!

GOOD.

SOON...

THE ROYAL CITY IS SECURE, GENERAL. IF THE DROIDS SEND A SECOND WAVE, WE'LL BE READY.

I'D LIKE TO KNOW WHY WE WEREN'T READY FOR THE FIRST ONE.

I'M JUST HAPPY YOU GOT HERE WHEN YOU DID. IT'S GOOD TO SEE YOU, OLD FRIEND.

YOU DON'T KNOW?

AGREED. WHERE IS *PRINCE YOJAN*, THOUGH -- SHOULDN'T *HE* BE DEFENDING THE CITY?

HE HAS *LEFT* US.

MY SON HAS JOINED THE SEPARATISTS.

HE'S WORKING WITH THE DROIDS TO BUILD SOME KIND OF SUPERWEAPON...ONE THAT WILL DRIVE THE REPUBLIC *AWAY* FROM OUR PLANET.

THAT DOESN'T SOUND LIKE THE YOJAN I KNOW.

IT *DOES* SOUND LIKE I NEED TO GO KNOCK SOME SENSE INTO HIM.

THAT'S ALWAYS YOUR WAY, ISN'T IT? BEND SOMETHING TO YOUR WILL EVEN IF YOU *BREAK* IT IN THE PROCESS.

PERHAPS YOJAN IS THE ONLY ONE OF US WHO IS THINKING *CLEARLY.*

HOW DO YOU FIGURE *THAT?*

HIGHNESS, WITH RESPECT -- YOU'RE NOT MAKING ANY SENSE. YOU'VE ALWAYS BEEN AN *ALLY* TO THE REPUBLIC. I DON'T UNDERSTAND --

AND I CONTINUE TO BE AN ALLY, I PROMISE YOU. IT'S JUST THAT...

...I'D HOPED THE WAR WOULD END BEFORE SIMOCADIA WAS FORCED TO CHOOSE A SIDE.

IT'S FUNNY, ISN'T IT? WE'RE A WORLD OF ARTISTS -- OF STONECUTTERS. OF WHAT INTEREST ARE *WE* TO THE REST OF THE GALAXY?

BUT THE TORCHES WE USE TO CUT THOSE STONES AND MAKE THIS ART -- THE TOOLS OF OUR PEACEFUL TRADE -- ARE WHAT *DOOMED* US.

IT'S THE *AGROCITE* THAT POWERS THEM. IT'S A VALUABLE -- AND SCARCE -- RESOURCE FOR WEAPONS BUILDING. SIMOCADIA IS ONE OF THE FEW WORLDS RICH WITH IT.

YES, BUT THERE WAS NO TIME TO UNDERSTAND WHAT WE HAD --

"-- THE REPUBLIC BROKERED EXCLUSIVE MINING RIGHTS AND BEGAN DRILLING IMMEDIATELY.

"IT WAS OBSCENE.

"THE DROID HORDES QUICKLY FOLLOWED, STAKING THEIR OWN CLAIM TO THE VALUABLE ORE, AND SOON IT WAS ALL-OUT *WAR*."

WE'VE LOST SO MUCH ALREADY.

I KNOW, BUT IT'S NOT TOO LATE. WHATEVER DROVE YOJAN TO THE OTHER SIDE CAN BE *UNDONE*.

YOU STILL DON'T UNDERSTAND.

IS IT TRUE THAT THE JEDI AREN'T ALLOWED TO MARRY?

YES. FORMING ATTACHMENTS IS DISCOURAGED.

SO NO CHILDREN THEN, EITHER?

NO.

26

THAT'S A SHAME. THE BOND BETWEEN A PARENT AND THEIR CHILD IS ONE OF THE MOST PRECIOUS THINGS IN THE GALAXY.

WITHOUT HAVING FELT THAT, THERE'S NO WAY YOU CAN KNOW WHAT I'M GOING THROUGH...OR HOW I CAN SO EASILY FORGIVE MY SON'S TRANSGRESSIONS.

I'M A *JEDI*, HIGHNESS -- NOT A ROBOT.

WE *DO* FEEL EMOTION.

SUPPRESSING YOUR EMOTIONS IS NOT THE SAME AS *FEELING* THEM, MACE. YOU'VE CHANGED SO MUCH SINCE YOU WERE LAST HERE.

THE JEDI HAVE HELPED YOU TAME THE TEMPEST INSIDE OF YOU... BUT THEY'VE ALSO COOLED YOUR PASSION.

I DON'T HAVE TIME FOR THIS.

WHAT DOES *ANY* OF THIS HAVE TO DO WITH WHY YOJAN HAS BETRAYED US...OR WHY THAT DOESN'T BOTHER YOU?

27

YOU DON'T KNOW WHAT YOU'RE TALKING ABOUT. WE'RE HERE TO *END* THE FIGHTING -- TO BRING *PEACE* AND *BALANCE* TO YOUR WORLD.

THAT WILL NEVER HAPPEN AS LONG AS EVERYONE WANTS A PIECE OF OUR PLANET.

I DON'T KNOW WHAT MY SON IS DOING, BUT I *TRUST* HIM... EVEN IF YOU CAN'T UNDERSTAND WHY.

THEN YOU KNOW I'M DUTY BOUND TO STOP HIM. WITH OR WITHOUT YOUR CONSENT.

IT IS MOST DEFINITELY *WITHOUT.*

MY SON IS AS STUBBORN AS YOU ARE, MACE. IF YOU GO AFTER HIM -- ONE OF YOU IS AS GOOD AS DEAD.

SHE'S RIGHT, I'M AFRAID. WE CAN'T LET YOU LEAVE.

YOU REALLY THINK YOU CAN STOP ME?

NO...

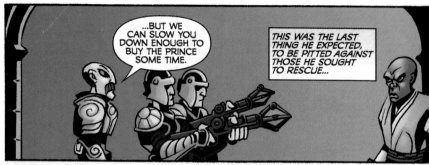

...BUT WE CAN SLOW YOU DOWN ENOUGH TO BUY THE PRINCE SOME TIME.

THIS WAS THE LAST THING HE EXPECTED, TO BE PITTED AGAINST THOSE HE SOUGHT TO RESCUE...

FWOOM! FWOOM!

KZZZM!

...THOUGH IT'S DISAPPOINTMENT HE FEELS, RATHER THAN SURPRISE...

KZASH!

...AS ENTIRE WORLDS STRAIN UNDER THE WEIGHT OF THESE CLONE WARS, WHAT HOPE DO FRIENDSHIPS -- SUCH FRAGILE THINGS -- HAVE OF SURVIVING?

It wasn't his fight to wage, this young stranger -- but he threw himself into battle to save our world ... thinking nothing of his own life.

Such headstrong and youthful vigor... Sometimes that ALONE is enough to carry one to victory.

Sometimes.

I CAN'T *BELIEVE* THIS. THE REPUBLIC'S HERE TO *HELP* YOU. *I'M* HERE TO HELP YOU.

YOU'RE *WRONG,* EMPRESS -- ABOUT THE JEDI, AND ABOUT ME. I'LL BRING YOUR SON BACK --*ALIVE.*

IN THE MEANTIME I SUGGEST YOU THINK LONG AND HARD ABOUT DOING WHAT'S *RIGHT* FOR THIS PLANET.

JEDI -- WAIT!

I CAN HELP YOU!

HELP ME -- OR DISTRACT ME AGAIN?

LOOK AT ME... YOU THINK I'D BE ABLE TO HOLD YOU BACK FOR EVEN A SECOND?

THEN SPEAK OR GET OUT OF MY WAY.

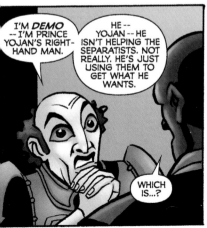

I'M *DEMO* -- I'M PRINCE YOJAN'S RIGHT-HAND MAN.

HE -- YOJAN -- HE ISN'T HELPING THE SEPARATISTS. NOT REALLY. HE'S JUST USING THEM TO GET WHAT HE WANTS.

WHICH IS...?

TO *DESTROY* THE AGROCITE MINES AND ANYONE NEAR THEM.

HE'S LOST HIS MIND -- YOU HAVE TO STOP HIM.

"EONS AGO, IN AN AGE BEFORE OUR OWN, ANOTHER SPECIES RULED SIMOCADIA. AN ADVANCED CULTURE THAT SUDDENLY AND MYSTERIOUSLY VANISHED.

"OUR SCHOLARS ARE OBSESSED WITH THEM. SO IS YOJAN.

"WE DON'T KNOW MUCH ABOUT THEM ... BUT WHAT LITTLE WE'VE PIECED TOGETHER SAYS THAT THEY FOUGHT THEIR WARS USING THE *ARDANA SHADEX.*

"STONE GIANTS THAT COULD TOPPLE MOUNTAINS!"

KROOM!

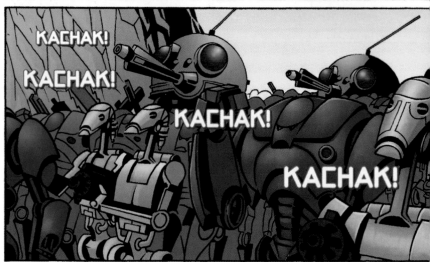

SHORTLY, NOT FAR AWAY...

BE CAREFUL WITH THAT!

PRISONER TRANSPORT. I'M SUPPOSED TO HAND HIM OVER TO PRINCE YOJAN DIRECTLY.

DON'T WORRY -- HE'S LOCKED UP TIGHT.

SEE?

YOU'VE EXHAUSTED A PLANET'S WORTH OF BANKING-CLAN CREDITS ON THIS OPERATION-- WHEN DO WE GET TO SEE WHAT WE'VE PAID FOR?!

YOU'LL SEE IT SOON ENOUGH, *ORRIN.* AND TRUST ME, IT'LL BE WORTH EVERY CREDIT--

WHAT ABOUT EVERY DROP OF BLOOD YOU'LL SPILL--

WHAT ARE YOU *DOING* OUT HERE, YOJAN? WHY DIDN'T YOU CONTACT ME BEFORE THINGS GOT THIS OUT OF CONTROL?

BECAUSE I KNEW IT WOULDN'T CHANGE ANYTHING. OUR FRIENDSHIP HOLDS STRONG, BUT OUR LOYALTIES NO LONGER ALIGN.

BECAUSE I KNEW YOU WOULD TRY TO STOP ME.

BUT ALL OF THIS...IT'S BEYOND REASON. YOU'D DESTROY YOUR OWN PLANET TO SAVE IT?

YOU HAVE TO END THIS MADNESS.

KKKKZZZHH!

"The stranger came to save us," the empress told her son.

"We cannot let him fall."

"We pledge our lives to this," the prince replied.

"We'll return with him safely ... or we will not return at all."

ZAK!

MY HEART SANK WHEN I HEARD YOU'D ARRIVED.

I'D ALWAYS HOPED YOU'D RETURN, BUT I NEVER WANTED IT TO BE LIKE THIS.

I'M NOT TOO HAPPY ABOUT IT, EITHER. BUT HOW IT PLAYS OUT IS UP TO YOU.

IF YOU WANT TO DO WHAT'S BEST FOR THIS PLANET-- YOU'LL *YIELD.*

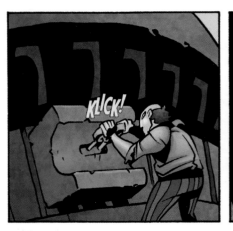

NO!

50

COME ON, COME ON -- *START!*

QUICK-- GET ON THAT SHIP!

RRRRRRERRARRRN!

TAKE MY HAND! REACH FOR IT!

THERE HAS TO BE A WAY TO DEACTIVATE IT.

THERE *WAS...*UNTIL YOU DESTROYED IT.

DEMO -- GO TAKE THE CONTROLS FROM THAT NEIMOIDIAN. BRING US AROUND AS CLOSE TO THE ARDANA SHADEX AS YOU CAN.

I'M ON IT.

IF WE CAN RETRIEVE THE *GLASS KEY* -- IF IT'S NOT TOO BADLY DAMAGED -- THERE MAY STILL BE A CHANCE...

With great effort, the prince and his companions fought their way through the enemy hordes...

... unsure even if the stranger was still alive.

But he was.

Together the young stranger, the prince, and his allies prepared to face the greatest challenge of their lives...

... confident in their combined strengths -- never for a moment doubting that their victory was at hand...

NEARBY...

IT'S WORKING, LIEUTENANT -- WE HAVE THEM ON THE RUN!

KROOM!

HHGNRRAAGH!!

WHAT IS *THAT?!*

DID YOU JUST SAY "*GET INSIDE*" OF THAT THING?

UNFORTUNATELY, YES. IT'S THE ONLY WAY WE CAN STOP IT.

"ITS CREATORS HID A KILL SWITCH DEEP WITHIN ITS BODY."

"EASY FOR *THEM* TO REACH, BUT PROTECTED FROM ANY ENEMIES THAT WOULD ATTEMPT TO ACCESS IT."

YOU MEAN LIKE *WE'RE* ABOUT TO DO.

GETTING TO IT IS THE EASY PART...GETTING BACK OUT *ALIVE* WILL BE NEXT TO IMPOSSIBLE.

I'LL DO IT. "*IMPOSSIBLE*" IS MY SPECIALTY.

NO, MACE...

...YOU EXACERBATED THIS SITUATION, BUT I *CREATED* IT. AWAKENING THAT MONSTROSITY WAS *MY* DOING.

I'VE ENDANGERED MY PEOPLE, AND HONOR DEMANDS THAT *I* PUT THIS RIGHT.

WE CAN SPLIT HAIRS OVER WHOSE FAULT THIS IS *LATER.*

I PROMISED THE EMPRESS THAT I'D BRING YOU BACK *ALIVE* -- THAT DOESN'T MEAN LETTING YOU JUMP HEADLONG INTO CERTAIN DEATH.

WHATEVER YOU TWO DECIDE TO DO, YOU'D BETTER DO IT *FAST* --

"-- THAT THING'S HEADED FOR THE ROYAL CITY!"

WE NEED TO GET THE GLASS KEY FROM THE INHIBITOR ON THE BEAST'S NECK. *I* NEED *YOU* TO GET THE KEY *FOR* ME.

MACE, PLEASE...THIS REQUIRES *BOTH* OF US. DO YOU UNDERSTAND?

DEMO -- BRING US IN CLOSE! CLOSE ENOUGH TO SMELL ITS BREATH!

THANK YOU, MY FRIEND.

SO HERE IT IS, MACE THINKS... THE INEVITABLE OUTCOME OF LETTING HIS EMOTIONS GET THE BETTER OF HIM. AGAIN.

SO QUICK TO RUN INTO BATTLE, SO QUICK TO SAVE THE DAY.

SO QUICK TO SWING A SABER WHEN A CALM CONVERSATION MIGHT HAVE ENDED THE CONFLICT.

THINGS START OUT DIFFERENTLY, BUT THEY *ALWAYS* END THE SAME.

COME ON!

SO WHY THEN IS IT THE HARDEST LESSON TO LEARN?

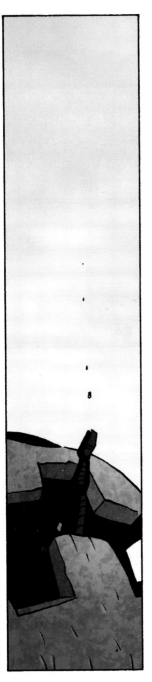

MACE --!

I CAN'T GET OUT! I CAN'T GET OUT!

YOJAN -- HANG ON!

Our enemies never stood a chance.

Utterly vanquished, the invaders returned whence they came, vowing to never again attack our home.

The prince and the stranger did more than save our people that day...

LATER...

CLEANUP IS UNDERWAY, GENERAL. WE SHOULD HAVE THAT THING CHOPPED AND SLABBED IN NO TIME.

THE TECHNOLOGY IS...INTERESTING, UNIQUE. WE MAY BE ABLE TO UTILIZE SOME OF IT.

AND THE PRINCE...?

"HIS BODY WAS JUST RECOVERED, SIR.

"HE...DIDN'T MAKE IT. I'M SORRY."

YOU WERE RIGHT, MASTER YODA.

I SHOULD NEVER HAVE COME HERE. I LET MY FEELINGS GET IN THE WAY. I ACTED RASHLY.

"I WAS A *HERO* TO THESE PEOPLE, AND NOW THEY *HATE* ME. FAIR OR NOT, I'M BLAMED FOR EVERYTHING THAT'S HAPPENED...

"...INCLUDING THE PRINCE'S DEATH.

"MY RELATIONSHIP WITH THE EMPRESS IS FOREVER *BROKEN*."

TRUE WERE YOUR INTENTIONS. KNOW THAT *THIS* WOULD BE THE OUTCOME, YOU COULD NOT.

TRAGIC, IT IS...BUT IN *VAIN* YOUR EFFORTS WERE NOT.

74

"SCATTERED ARE THE SEPARATIST FORCES. DRIVEN BACK, THEY HAVE BEEN.

"*SAFE* IN REPUBLIC HANDS, SIMOCADIA IS NOW.

"ALSO MUCH TO LEARN, WE HAVE, FROM THE COLOSSUS YOU FELLED.

"AN EXTRAORDINARY MACHINE, IT IS."

IF THIS IS A VICTORY, IT SURE FEELS *HOLLOW.* THE MOSCIVE RESENT OUR PRESENCE -- THEY DON'T WANT US HERE.

THEY THINK WE HAVE TAKEN CONTROL OF THEIR LAND AND -- BY CLAIMING OWNERSHIP OF THE COLOSSUS -- THAT WE'VE STOLEN A PIECE OF THEIR HISTORY.

IS *THIS* WHAT THE WAR HAS COME TO?

ALSO AVAILABLE NOW:

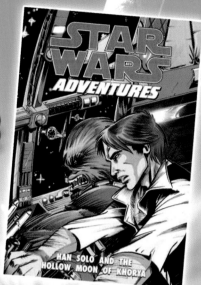

HAN SOLO AND THE
HOLLOW MOON OF KHORYA

ISBN: 9781845769055

PRINCESS LEIA AND
THE ROYAL RANSOM

BN: 9781845769550

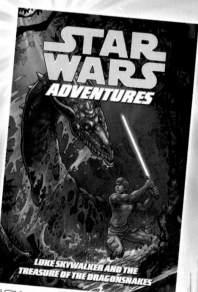

LUKE SKYWALKER AND THE
TREASURE OF THE DRAGONSNAKES

ISBN: 9781848564008

WWW.TITANBOOKS.COM
WWW.STARWARS.COM

THE FORCE IS

www.titanbooks.com

DON'T MISS THE CONTINUING BATTLE AGAIN
CLONE WARS